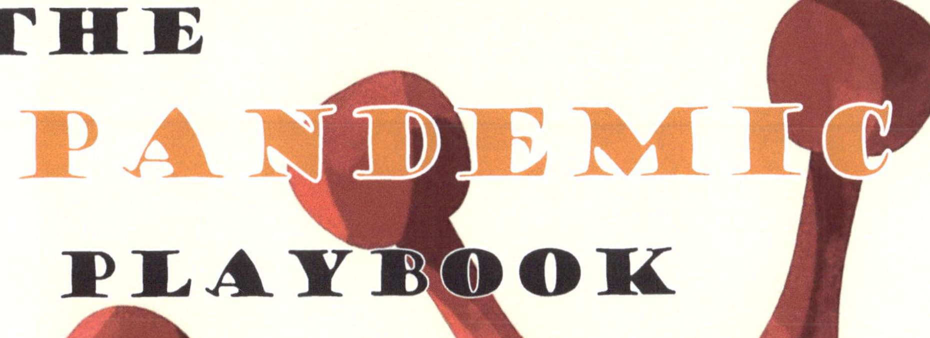

# THE PANDEMIC PLAYBOOK

## A Game Plan to Stay Safe

Lisa Stewart

# DEDICATION

To my children, Trey, Elisabeth, Anne Marie, and Marissa


To parents and children everywhere
Learning is a lifelong process, and we must learn from science in order to advance.


Thank you to my students of the past and present
You teach me so much more than I could ever teach you!


To Julie, Jessica, Chandra, Maddox, Bob, Sarah, Logan, Stacy, Matt, Billy, Davis, Tom, and Brandon
Thank you for your friendship and support.

iv.

# ACKNOWLEDGMENTS

Thank you to my mother, Marlene Hatton, my first educator. Without you, I would not be the person I am today. Thank you to my father, Duane Hatton, for being my biggest fan. You supported me throughout life's darkest moments, even when no one else did. Thank you for your superb editing, Billy Stewart. You kept me going, edited my work continuously, and your encouragement is the reason I never gave up. To my friends and colleagues, your contributions were crucial in solidifying the content of this book. Thank you, Matt Deimling. Your knowledge of infectious diseases is invaluable, and this project would not have been a success without your guidance and editing. Thank you to Chandra Moon, Maddox Moon, and Dr. Bob Hennigan for fact-checking the content and recommending critical edits that directed the project's path. To my friend, Dr. Robert Keyes, Thank you for verifying the medical efficacy and editing the book's content. Thank you, Brandon. I appreciate your input, love, and support as an author, as my equal, and always as my baby brother. Thank you, Tom Jones, my other brother. You promised not to go easy on me when you reviewed this book, and your stamp of approval means the world to me! Thank you for your input, love, and support. Trey, your opinions on the illustrations and assistance in editing them were extremely beneficial. Your information gave the entire book a different look. Thank you, Davis Chu, for your talented artistic renderings. The cover illustrations and design are outstanding! Lastly, thank you to my colleagues and administrators in the Hamilton City School District, where I have the privilege of serving the students and their families.

The Coronavirus

Pandemic affects people
everywhere, and it is
essential to understand
who is being affected,
what is happening,
why it is happening,
and how to live safely!
I bet you have A LOT
of questions.
I sure do.
Let's explore together!

# I WONDER

What are an epidemic and a pandemic?

Who are the experts?

What information should we trust?

What types of diseases cause a pandemic?

What has history taught us about diseases and pandemics?

How do we use what we have learned from the past to help keep us safe?

Science is the act of exploring and learning about the world around us by questioning, observing, researching, experimenting, and recording the facts.

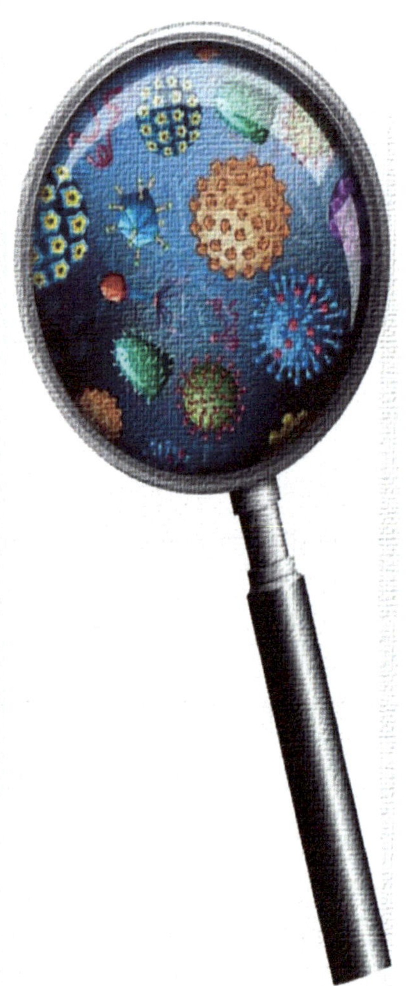

An **infectious disease** is a disease that spreads from one person to another. When it spreads quickly, it becomes difficult to control and can sweep across an area rapidly. When this happens, an infectious disease becomes an epidemic or a pandemic.

A disease is considered to be an **epidemic** when there is an increase in the number of cases, and it spreads very quickly among people. It spreads more rapidly than scientists would expect.

A **pandemic** is the most severe type of epidemic. It is a disease that affects a large area, like a country, a continent, or the entire world.

**FUN FACT:** The word pandemic was first recorded around 1660. It comes from the Latin word pandēmus and the Greek word pándēmos. "Pan" means all or every, and "demos" means people. Since pandemics existed long before that time, many historians believe that people have been studying them since ancient times.

# What sources of information can we trust?

There is so much information available about diseases. Some of the information is conflicting, and this can be confusing. How do we know what information we can trust?

Before people recorded information, stories were passed down through history by word of mouth from generation to generation. One example of this is folktales. These stories are often not reliable sources of information.

It is important to trust **reliable sources** for accurate information. A reliable source means that the experts provide information based on proven facts, and it is **unbiased** or not the writer's opinion.

**Who's WHO?** We celebrate World Health Day on April 7th every year because the World Health Organization, known as WHO, began on April 7, 1948. The organization consists of scientists and experts from around the world. Their goal is to keep the world safe from diseases and to help all people have good, quality healthcare. So, who are the experts?

# Who are the experts?

Most important, we should trust the experts. Pandemics and epidemics are studied and overcome by scientists, who are called **epidemiologists**. Epidemiologists are the experts.

Epidemiologists study diseases in humans. They analyze what caused epidemics that have occurred throughout history. By learning from the past, epidemiologists prepare for diseases that may arise in the future and to prevent them from becoming epidemics or pandemics.

**FUN FACT:** Did you notice that epidemic and epidemiologist are similar words? The word epidemiologist was first used and defined in the 1800s. It means one who studies the science of epidemics.

How does someone become an expert?

# How does someone become an epidemiologist?

When someone graduates from high school, they receive a **diploma**. A diploma is a certificate that proves that someone has completed all of the necessary classes in high school. A **degree** is a diploma for college students. A degree demonstrates that a college student has completed all of the courses needed to work in a particular career.

In order to become an epidemiologist, someone must study for approximately seven years in college.  The degrees that people earn to work in this field are in biology, medicine, public health, or one of the other science degrees. What do the experts do?

**Biology is the science of living things.**

**Chemistry is the science of matter and the changes it can undergo.**

**Public Health is the science of keeping people healthy.**

# The Scientific Method

It is essential to understand that scientists use a specific method that determines which discoveries work and which do not work. They use a process of investigation called the Scientific Method. Since ancient times, at least 3600 years ago, there have been men and women who studied science, math, and the way people think. Some of these people may sound familiar to you like, Aristotle, Plato, and Isaac Newton.

In 1620, Sir Francis Bacon wrote a book that organized and listed a system of steps that scientists use to prove whether a scientific idea is a fact or false. The steps he listed had been practiced for thousands of years and guided all scientific studies. He established how to prove whether or not scientific ideas or thoughts are correct. The method he identified and recorded is called the Scientific Method.

The Scientific Method is a process that uses science to examine, measure, and experiment to understand and learn if scientists can confirm ideas by testing them.

# Steps in the Scientific Method

**QUESTION** — **Ask a question.** The first step always begins with an unanswered scientific question. Who? What? When? Where? How? Why?

**RESEARCH** — **Research** by studying credible sources to learn as much as possible about the question.

**HYPOTHESIS** — **Create a hypothesis** or an educated guess to answer your question.

**EXPERIMENT** — **Conduct an experiment** to test your hypothesis.

**ANALYZE** — **Analyze the data** or information that you collected from the experiment that you performed.

**CONCLUSION** — **Form a conclusion** or answer the question posed at the beginning of the process.

# What types of diseases cause a pandemic?

Now that we understand what a pandemic is, who the experts are, and how the experts determine scientific facts, let's take a look at the types of diseases that have caused pandemics throughout history. Below is a timeline of the most notable pandemics and the number of deaths that occurred.

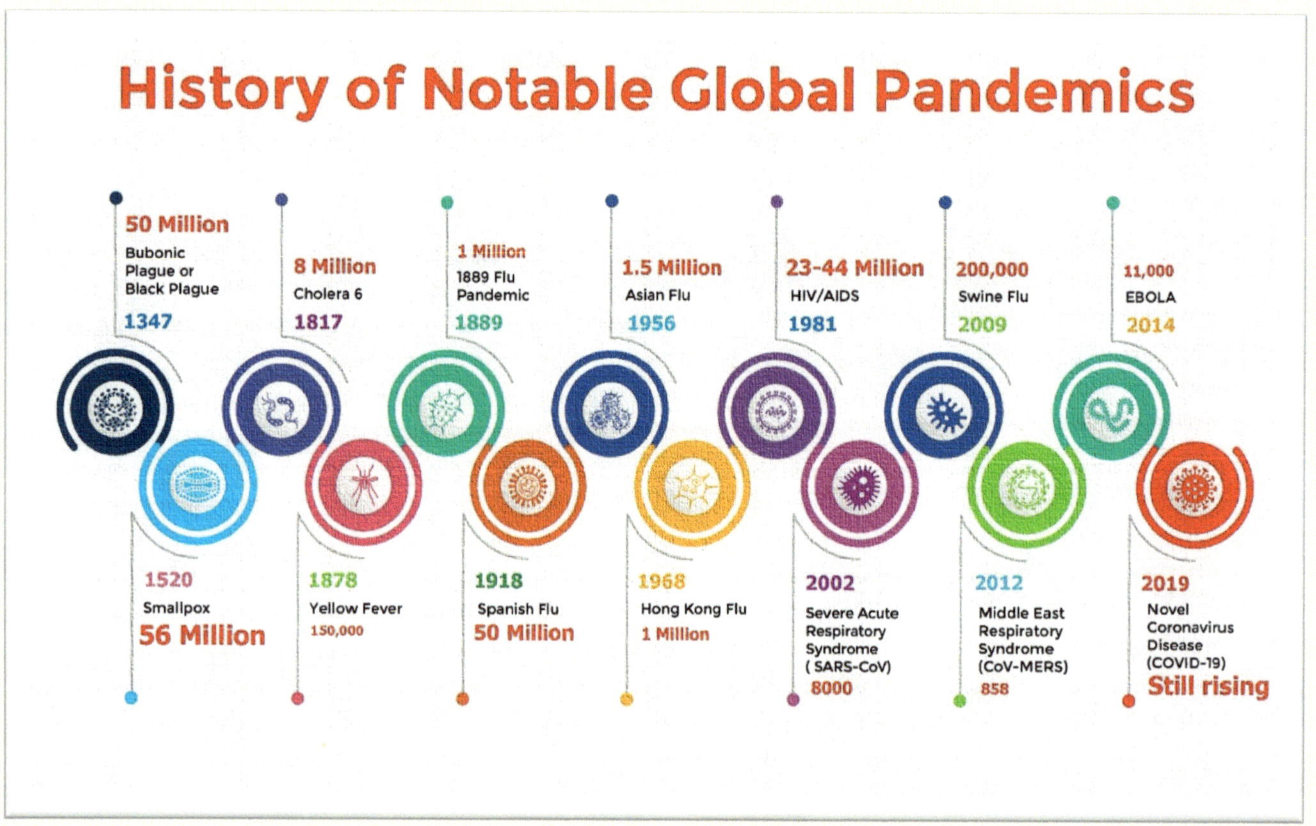



**WOW!** What does all that information mean? Let's walk through it step by step.

# Putting the Puzzle Pieces Together

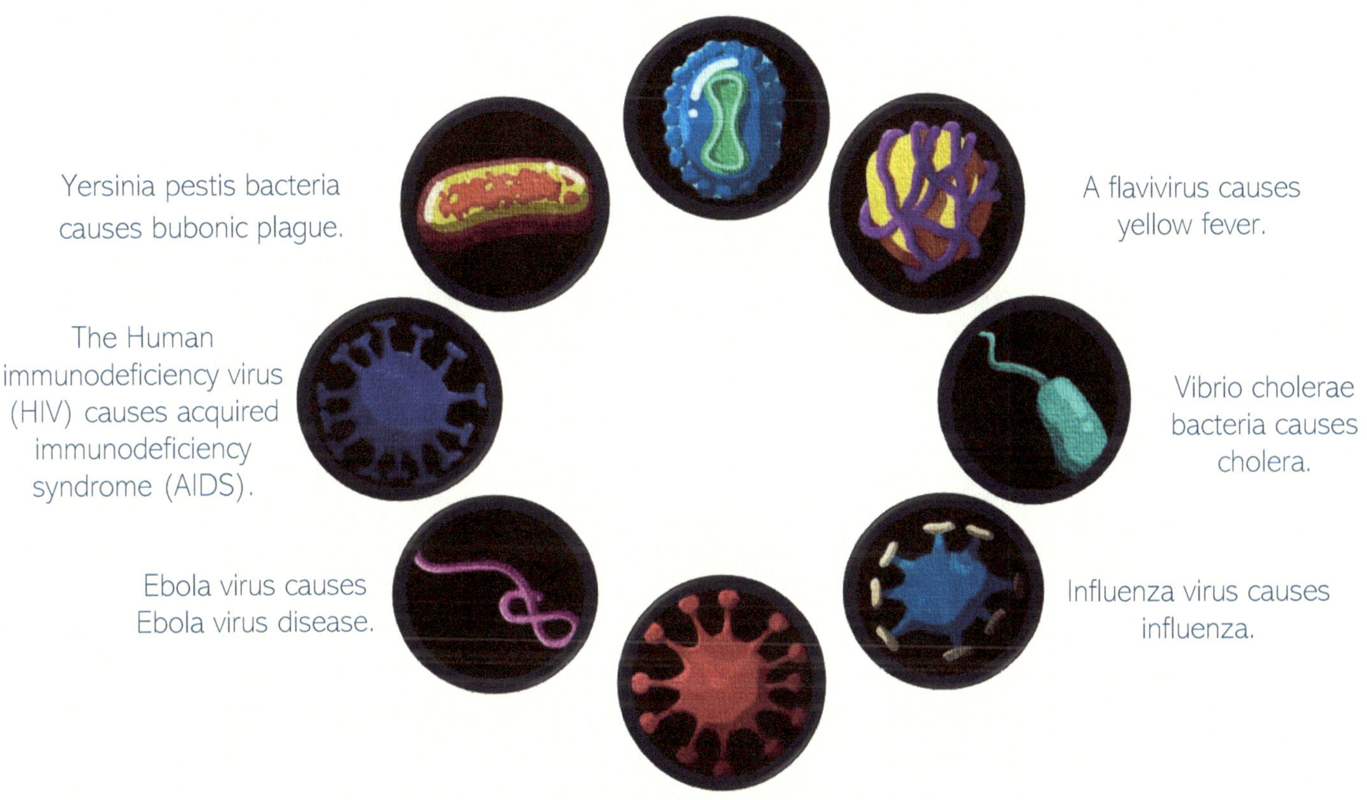

# What do we know about coronavirus?

We do not know much about COVID-19 because it is a new disease, but we are learning more every day. Coronavirus is not a new virus, though. There are actually seven known types of human coronaviruses, and it was first discovered in the 1960s. Three of the viruses have caused pandemics. The three coronaviruses that have become pandemics are:

- Middle Eastern respiratory syndrome or MERS,
- Severe acute respiratory syndrome or SARS, and
- Coronavirus disease 2019 or COVID-19.

The COVID-19 pandemic has affected the world. There is still so much that we do not know about this disease. One thing that is not clear is why some people have severe symptoms and others do not. We do know that the most common symptoms of COVID-19 are fever and cough.

We do not know for sure how humans originally became infected with the coronavirus. We do know that humans transmit coronavirus to other humans, usually by coughing, sneezing, talking, or singing. Sometimes, animals also transmit diseases to humans. Let's take a look at some examples.

# What are zoonotic diseases?

Most of the diseases that have become pandemics were transmitted from animals to humans. When an animal spreads an infection to humans, it is called a **zoonotic disease**. It was given this name because it is transmitted from animals to humans. The prefix zoo- means having to do with animals.

The first Ebola epidemic occurred in 1976 in villages in Africa. Scientists suspect that fruit bats bit infected wild animals, who then transmitted Ebola to humans.  Humans can also spread Ebola to other humans.

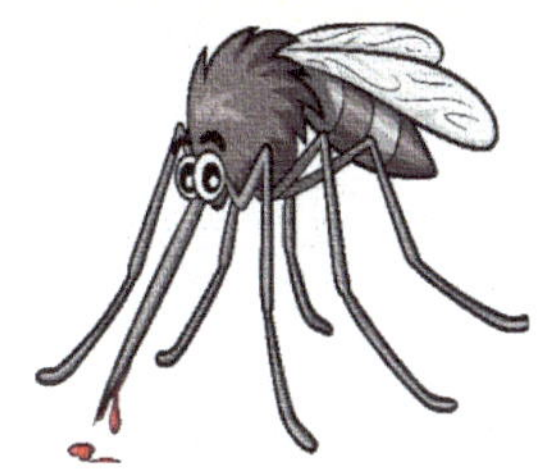

Yellow Fever has been around since the 1700s.  The first known epidemic occurred on the island of Barbados. A doctor named Walter Reed proved that mosquitoes transmitted yellow fever to humans around 1900. Infected mosquitoes transmit yellow fever to humans. Mosquitoes became infected from coming in contact with the blood of an infected animal.

Scientists believe that HIV transferred from animals to humans sometime around the early 1900s. In 1999, scientists traced HIV back to monkeys. The monkeys were infected with a virus called simian immunodeficiency virus or SIV, which is almost identical to HIV. Scientists believed that hunters either ate infected animals or came in contact with their infected blood.

How do we know what will help to prevent the coronavirus disease? What has history taught us about preventing diseases and pandemics? Let's take a look at some of the preventative measures that help prevent diseases from spreading.

Were you confused when school ended so quickly last spring, and people were required to stay in their homes? How did scientists know that this method would work to slow the spread of the coronavirus? The answer lies in the first major recorded pandemic in recent history. The bubonic plague often called the Black Death, demonstrated that quarantine is a scientifically proven method for slowing the spread of infectious diseases.

**Quarantine** is the practice of separating people from one another to control or stop an infectious disease from spreading. WHY do we use this practice today? Let's follow the scientist's steps of inquiry to determine how it was proven to be an effective prevention method.

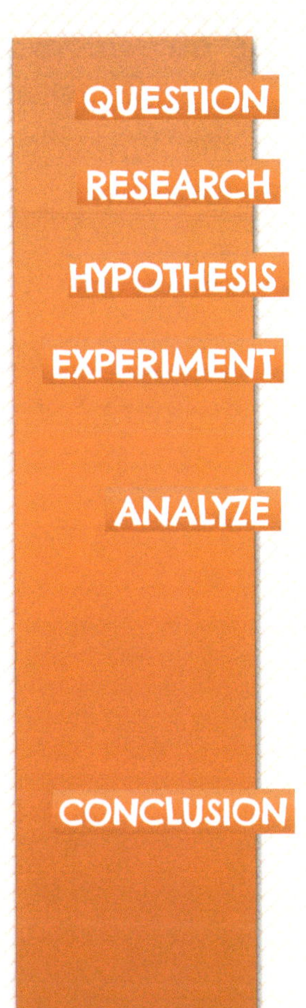


In 1347, scientists wondered why many people were suddenly becoming sick and dying during the bubonic plague. They could not find any physical evidence to explain how the illness was spreading.

Scientists believed that the air people were breathing was contaminated or causing people to become sick.

For this reason, everyone was forced to stay inside their homes.

The quarantine worked. The plague was better controlled, and fewer people were getting sick. After further research, scientists learned that the air was not contaminated after all.

The practice of quarantine worked to control the plague, although not for a reason scientists initially thought. The Black Plague was actually transmitted by fleas that bit black rats who were infected with the bacteria. People were infected when these fleas would bite humans. When people stayed inside their homes, they were not getting bitten by the fleas that carried the bacteria and, the disease did not spread.

The benefits of quarantine have been known since ancient times. It has become a scientifically proven method of controlling and stopping the spread of infectious diseases. For many years, the plague wiped out large populations, but now people can easily be treated with antibiotics or medicine.

The cholera epidemic made way for **contact tracing** to become an effective method for controlling diseases. Contact tracing is the practice of identifying people exposed to a virus to prevent sick people from spreading the illness to healthy people.

You may be thinking the same thing that I am: Why would anyone purposely spread a disease to others?

When someone is exposed to a bacteria or virus, they do not show symptoms immediately. It typically takes anywhere from days to a few weeks after a person becomes infected before experiencing symptoms.

So, people spread the disease without realizing it.

For example, suppose you are infected with a virus on Monday morning, and you play with your friend on Monday afternoon. In that case, your friend may become infected with the virus before you experience any symptoms.

And, when you go home, your family members can become infected.

Then, your family members and your friend's family members can spread the infection to their friends without knowing that they are infected. The pattern continues even before you show any symptoms of the disease.

How do scientists determine where a disease originated or began? Read this interesting story! It explains a lot about contact tracing.

When the first significant cholera epidemic began, scientists were unsure of how people were getting sick. And physicians were at a loss of what to do! After investigating what was going on and researching the situation, scientists thought people were breathing contaminated air. They tried many treatments that were not scientifically proven in the hopes of finding something that worked.

**QUESTION**

**RESEARCH**

When a doctor named John Snow was unsure that the cause of cholera was due to breathing contaminated air, he decided to question this thinking.

He used his medical knowledge to think critically about why people might be infected with a disorder that affects the intestines. It was more logical to believe that people were eating or drinking something that caused them to become sick. He also observed that people in Birmingham, a city where the residents do not drink well water, were not getting sick.

Dr. Snow believed that cholera was coming from dirty drinking water. He noticed that people who lived in Birmingham did not drink well water because it was dirty, and Birmingham did not have a cholera outbreak.

A few years later, there was a cholera outbreak in a small area in London. Several people died in a short period. Dr. Snow used a map of the city and tracked all the cholera cases. He was able to follow all the people infected with cholera to a single water pump.

After tracking the infected people to the water pump, he proved to city officials that it was most likely the water pump responsible for the cholera outbreak. They promptly removed the pump handle, and the epidemic was suddenly controlled.

Dr. Snow proved that his hypothesis was correct, and contact tracing was a scientifically proven to be an effective prevention method for controlling infectious diseases.

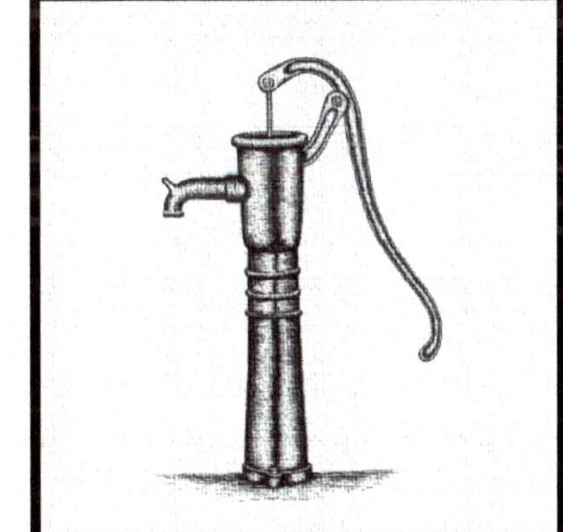

Have you ever wondered why going to the doctor and getting those pesky little **vaccines** or shots are so important? Well, believe it or not, they have their origins in a severe pandemic.

**Smallpox** is a disease that causes a rash with small bumps. The bumps are filled with fluid. These bumps are called **pocks**. When the pocks dry up, the person is left with scabs that turn into scars. Smallpox is transmitted from person to person when an infected person comes in contact with a healthy person. Smallpox is also transmitted when a healthy person comes in contact with an infected person's fluids or scabs.

# Fun Facts About Smallpox

Historians suspect that the first cases of smallpox existed as early as the 15th Century BCE. Archaeologists found a similar rash on three mummies in Egypt.

The word vaccine comes from the Latin word "Vacca," which means cow.

A doctor named Edward Jenner was ultimately credited with helping to end smallpox while in medical school. The story sure is exciting.

**QUESTION**

Dr. Jenner wondered if there was a way to cure smallpox.

**RESEARCH**

He learned that cowpox, a similar disease in cows, caused these same pocks on cow's udders. Dr. Jenner noticed that milkmaids who **contracted** or became sick with cowpox did not contract smallpox. He wondered why this was the case.

**HYPOTHESIS**

Dr. Jenner observed that the milkmaids who had exposure to cowpox seemed to have **immunity** or protection from smallpox.

He tested his theory by taking the fluid from a cow pock and infected an 8-year-old boy with the virus that caused cowpox. The boy had a small reaction to the virus, but the pocks quickly disappeared. He then exposed the boy to the virus that caused smallpox, and the boy had no reaction.

After analyzing the data, doctors all over the world used this same technique, and the number of new cases of smallpox declined.

Jenner's technique worked, and the vaccine was born! This vaccine was the first of many to control diseases. There are no new cases of smallpox in the world today, thanks to the widespread use of the vaccine.

**FUN FACT:** The last incident of smallpox occurred in 1977 in Somalia. Since then, there have been no cases of smallpox. In other words, smallpox has been **eradicated** or no longer exists because so many people around the world received the vaccine.

The influenza pandemic of 1918 taught us many lessons that we use today to help control the coronavirus. Like coronavirus, influenza, or flu is a disease that affects the lungs, and the way people breathe. Flu is transmitted from person to person. When a person with the virus talks, coughs, sneezes, or sings near a healthy person, the germs from the sick person's body can infect a healthy person. These germs can infect a healthy person that is standing nearby or by landing on surfaces. When a healthy person touches that surface, they can catch the infection, as well.

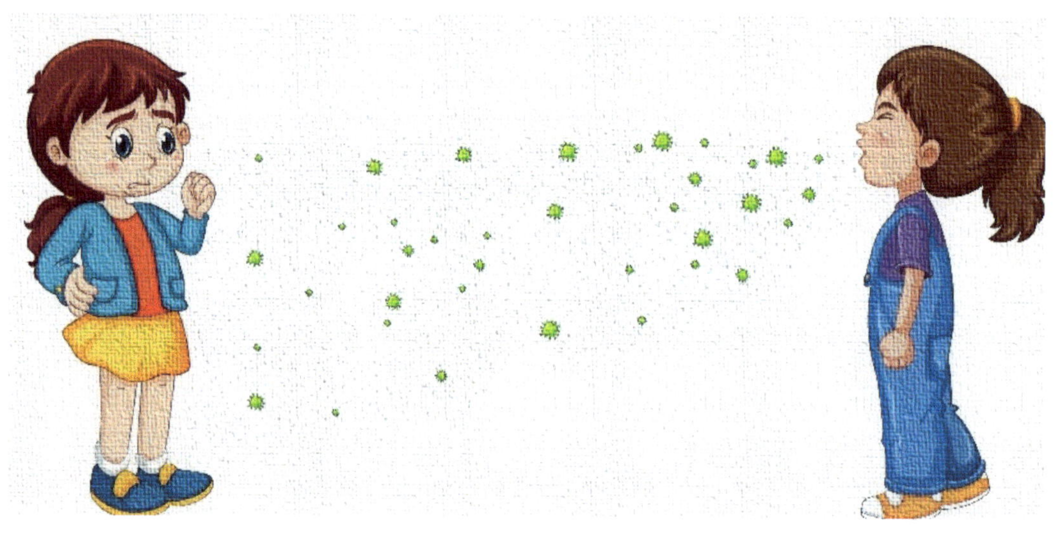

 **Social Distancing** is the practice of staying 6 feet away from one another. By keeping distance between yourself and others, you are doing your part to ensure that you do not spread germs before you show symptoms.

 **Sanitizing** is the practice of cleaning surfaces with a cleaning product that kills germs. Examples of surfaces include tables, chairs, doorknobs, sinks, etc. Doing this helps to keep areas clean so that people are less likely to become infected with a bacteria or virus when they touch that surface.

**Face coverings** are masks or some sort of material that covers your mouth and nose. The reason why face coverings are essential is that it limits the number of germs put into the air by each person during a pandemic.

**Hand washing** protects you and others by ensuring that, if you are infected with a virus or bacteria, you do not spread it to healthy people by touching your eyes, nose, or mouth and then touching a surface. Also, if you touch a surface that is contaminated with a virus or bacteria, then you can become infected yourself. So, for these reasons, it is particularly important to wash your hands regularly.

# Based on what you have learned, how can you be responsible members of your family, community, and world?

Monitor your health! Stay home if you do not feel well.

Keep your distance from others and use face coverings to prevent the virus's spread when you talk, cough, sneeze or sing.

Wash your hands often to protect yourself and others from the spread of viruses or bacteria.

Sanitize items and surfaces to help keep the area around you clean and free from germs. Parents or caregivers will often do this.

The coronavirus disease pandemic that we are experiencing is new to the world. Epidemiologists are trying to answer any and all questions about this very new disease to keep us safe. As they learn more about the coronavirus and attempt to control or end the pandemic, epidemiologists will continue to learn, just as the scientists have done in the past. They will learn from their mistakes to improve the way that we control diseases in the future.

Everyone in the world is experiencing this new situation together. No one knows who will have mild, cold-like symptoms or who will become terribly sick.

Healthcare workers are risking their lives for others who have become extremely sick from the virus.

We, as responsible citizens, should show kindness and compassion to others. We can do this by following practices that will help prevent the spread of the coronavirus disease to others.